Spot and Mom

by Michael Nicholson
illustrated by Merrill Rainey

Practice Decodable 6

McGraw Hill Education

Bothell, WA • Chicago, IL • Columbus, OH • New York, NY

MHEonline.com

Send all inquiries to:
McGraw-Hill Education
8787 Orion Place
Columbus, OH 43240

ISBN: 978-0-02-145037-4
MHID: 0-02-145037-4

Printed in China.

8 9 10 11 12 DSS 27 26 25 24 23

Spot ran to the top.

On top, Spot had to stop.

On top, Mom ran past him.

Can Mom spot Spot?

Spot ran to Mom.

Mom can spot him.